US ARMY AIR ASSAULT & GENERAL SUPPORT HELICOPTER UNIT PATCHES
VOL 2: NATIONAL GUARD & RESERVE UNITS (2001-2021)

CW4 DAN McCLINTON (USA/RET)

OTHER BOOKS BY THE AUTHOR

MILITARY INSIGNIA

US ARMY AIR CAVALRY PATCHES (2001-2021)
US ARMY ATTACK HELICOPTER UNIT PATCHES (2001-2021)
US ARMY AIR ASSAULT & GENERAL SUPPORT HELICOPTER UNIT PATCHES (2001-2021) VOL 1

PHOTOGRAPHY

37 MONTHS: IMAGES FROM THREE COMBAT TOURS IN IRAQ

MILITARY HISTORY

CRAZYHORSE: FLYING APACHE ATTACK HELICOPTERS WITH THE 1ST CAVALRY DIVISION IN IRAQ (2006-2007)

TABLE of CONTENTS

INTRODUCTION

Welcome to the fourth book in the series of books featuring US Army Aviation Unit Patches that have been worn since 11 September 2001. This book will feature patches used by the National Guard and Reserve Assault and General Support Aviation units during the Global War on Terror (GWOT). For those that have been here for the whole ride, welcome back and for those that are looking into the strange world of aviators and their patches, welcome and thanks for buying this. I hope you get something out of it. In many ways this has been the most difficult of all the books in the series to put together. I say this not as an excuse but to thank two fellow collectors for their assistance. Without the extensive help of Alan Woods and Keith Stilwell this book would be literally half the size that it is.

I will tell you up front that this book is flawed. In the process of making this book I made a few decisions about what would be included and what would be left out. Prior to the US Army reorganizing itself around 2005, Medical Evacuation units often called MEDEVAC or DUSTOFF were aligned under the Medical Service Corps and served in the early stages of the GWOT using designations like the 1159th Medical Company of the New Hampshire Army National Guard (see below). All told there were 54 separate designations prior to the reorganization undertaken by the Army. To avoid even more confusion than there already is I made the choice to not include these patches in this book.

Likewise, prior to the great reorganization CH-47 units were not named using the regimental system that would come into use later (example above). Not only are these older patches becoming harder to acquire, but they also don't necessarily follow any established pattern, so it is extremely difficult to know if we are missing a patch or if one never existed in the first place. While there are definitely some cool designs worthy of celebration, I made the decision to leave that for someone else to do. If you are here hoping to see your patch and it falls in that category, I apologize but I had to draw the line somewhere.

While I understand that all National Guard units are intensely proud to represent their home state, the nature of deployments and how units were organized to support them has caused me to list units in order by their regimental affiliation and not by their home state. I hope the folks from 2-149th AVN and the people of my native state of Texas can forgive me for this.

As I have said in every edition of these books, I have made every effort to make these books as complete as possible. If I inadvertently left your patch out or a patch was placed with the wrong unit, it is entirely my fault and if you let me know I will endeavor to make the appropriate correction in any future editions. As always I thank you for reading and your continued support of this effort to preserve history.

AIR ASSAULT!
Dan (dngrpig@gmail.com)

2nd Battalion 104th Aviation Regiment "WINGED SUPPORT"

General Support Aviation Battalion, PA ARNG, Fort Indiantown Gap, Pennsylvania

Battalion and Task Force patches

A Company 2-104 AVN "BLACK SHEEP"

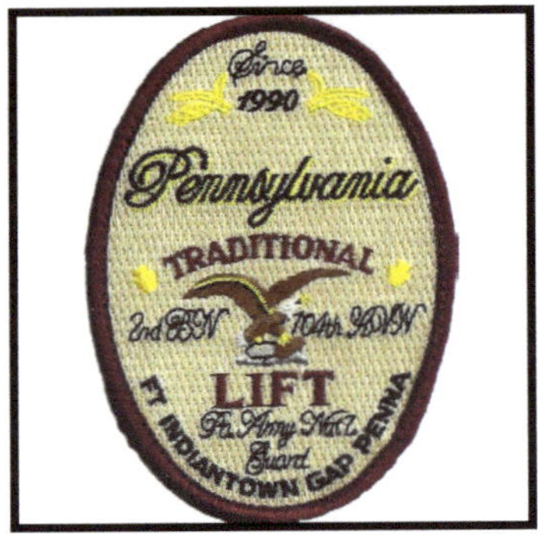

C Company 2-104 AVN "DUSTOFF"

TENNESSEE NATIONAL GUARD
SOUTHERN COMFORT
Det 1 Co 2-104th
DUSTOFF, SEARCH & RESCUE

TENNESSEE NATIONAL GUARD
SOUTHERN COMFORT
Det 1, Co 2/104th
DUSTOFF, SEARCH & RESCUE

OEF
WITCHDOCTOR OPS
2010-2011
C-2/104th AVN

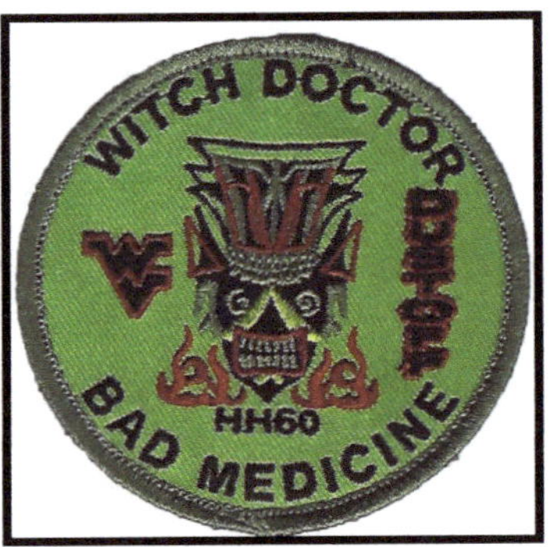
WITCH DOCTOR
WV
HH60
BAD MEDICINE

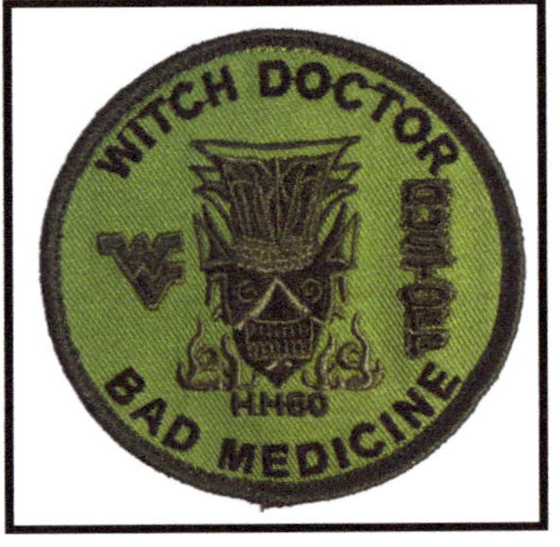
WITCH DOCTOR
WV
HH60
BAD MEDICINE

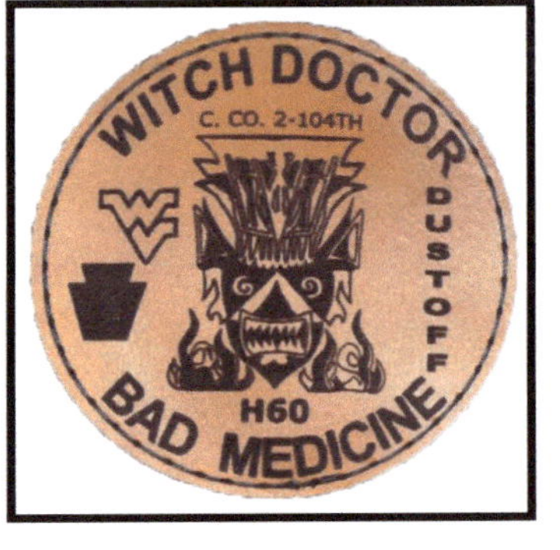
WITCH DOCTOR
C. CO. 2-104TH
DUSTOFF
H60
BAD MEDICINE

Since 2006
West Virginia
PREMIUM
MEDEVAC
AMERICA'S
FINEST HH-60 CO
C-2/104TH
Williamstown, WV

Since 2006
West Virginia
PREMIUM
MEDEVAC
AMERICA'S
FINEST HH-60 CO
C-2/104TH
Williamstown, WV

Det. 1
C CO. 2-104TH AVN
MEDEVAC
DUSTOFF
SAR
HH-60A - HH-60L

Det. 1
C CO. 2-104TH AVN
MEDEVAC
DUSTOFF
SAR
HH-60A - HH-60L

D CO.   2-104TH
BAT CLOWNS
ARE YOU AN IDIOT OR ARE YOU AN IDIOT?

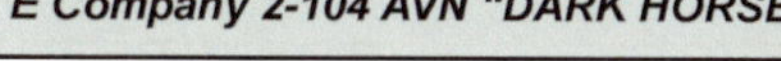

G Company 2-104 AVN

HHC 2-104 AVN

1st Battalion 106th Aviation Regiment "BLACKHORSE"

Assault Helicopter Battalion,

A Company 1-106 AVN "PHANTOMS"

B Company 1-106 AVN "MAD DOGS"

C Company 1-106 AVN "MUSTANGS"

E CO. 106TH AVN UNTOUCHABLES
CHICAGO, ILL

1st Battalion 108th Aviation Regiment "TALON"

Assault Helicopter Battalion,

Battalion and Task Force patches

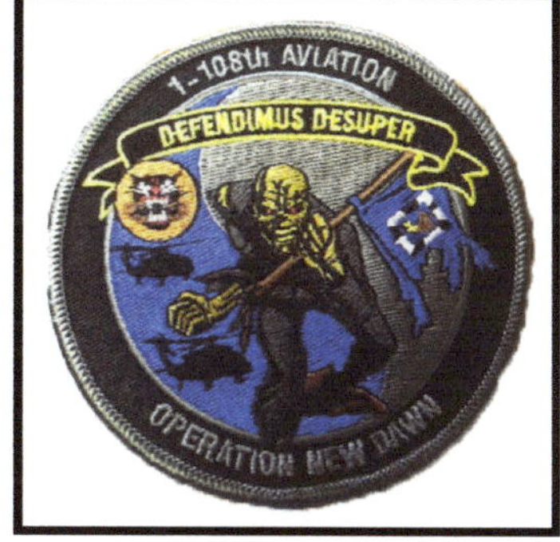

C Company 1-108 AVN

D Company 1-108 AVN

ECO 1-108TH AVN
KS-TX
"FEED THE BEAST"
OND 11-12
OUTCAST

HHC 1-108 AVN

HHC 1-108TH AVN
VIPER
BOSNIA-HERZEGOVINA SFOR 13
TASK FORCE WARRIOR

HHC 1-108TH AVN
OIF 09-10
WILDCATS

HHC 1-108TH AHB
RESULTS NOT EXCUSES

WE DEFEND
HHC
FROM ABOVE

Battalion and Task Force patches

B Company 1-111th AVN "BEASTMASTERS"

C Company 1-111 AVN "PAINKILLERS"

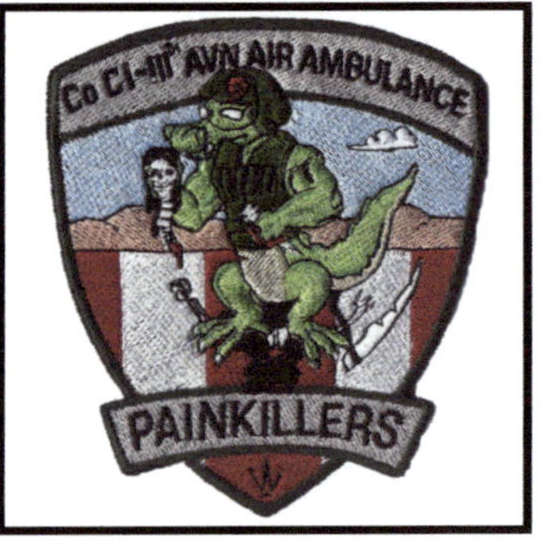

  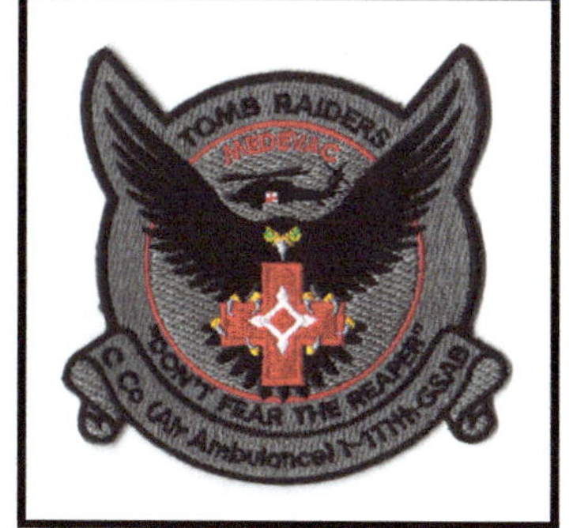  

D Company 1-111 AVN "BLACKSMITHS"

E Company 1-111 AVN

FREE STATE
DUSTOFF
G1-111
KS

FREE STATE
DUSTOFF
G1-111
KS

GENTLEMAN
GAMBLERS
G Co.
Tennessee
WE PLAY
FOR BLOOD
Dustoff

DET 2 CO G 1-111TH GSAB
WITHOUT HESITATION
ANYTIME ANYWHERE
WINDY CITY DUSTOFF

WITHOUT HESITATION, ANYTIME ANYWHERE
WINDY CITY

Task Force Wraith
C Co 2-149th
G Co 1-111th
1-147th AHB

1st Battalion 126th Aviation Regiment "DRAGONWING"

Battalion patches

A Co. 1-126 WOLFPACK
BROTHERHOOD OF THE WOLF

A Co. 1-126 WOLFPACK
BROTHERHOOD OF THE WOLF

A Co. 1-126 WOLFPACK
LE PACTE DES LOUPS

A Co. 1-126 WOLFPACK
LE PACTE DES LOUPS

DELTA SCHOONERS
B CO 1/126 AVN - STOCKTON CA

GOLD DIGGERS
OEF
B Co. 1-126TH AVN

B CO 1-126TH AVN CAARNG
ZEPHYR
ERBIL   TAJI
IRAQ 2018

ZEPHYR

B Co 1-126th GSAB
TF Liberty
Tail   Erbil
Zephyr
OIR 17 - 18 Iraq

MotherLode
Gold Diggers
SALERNO · SHANK · BAGRAM
CA   RNG
OEF XIII

motherlode
OPERATION ENDURING FREEDOM XIII

MOTHERLODE
"PUT SOME Ds ON IT"
OEF XII/XIII

BLACK MAGIC
B/6-101ST ★ B/1-126TH

DELAWARE DUSTOFF
DET. 1 C CO 1/126TH AVN

DELAWARE DUSTOFF
DET. 1 C CO 1/126TH AVN

MADE ON HONOR
RHODE ISLAND
Hi-Neighbor!
C Co 1-126th AVN
DUSTOFF
SOLD ON MERIT

THE FAMOUS
C Co 1-126th AVN
RHODE ISLAND
DUSTOFF

THE FAMOUS
C Co 1-126th AVN
RHODE ISLAND
DUSTOFF

DUSTOFF
KILLDEVILS
DET. 2   C-CO.
1-126TH

DUSTOFF
KILLDEVILS
DET. 2   C-CO.
1-126TH

C COMPANY 1-126TH MEDEVAC
RIDE
DUSTOFF
ANYONE ANYWHERE ANYTIME

C COMPANY 1-126TH MEDEVAC
RIDE
DUSTOFF
ANYONE ANYWHERE ANYTIME

BLACK BEAR
MEDEVAC
CO 1/126

BLACK BEAR MEDEVAC
Co. C1/126 AVN REGT. (AA)

HOPE DUSTOFF
CCo   1-126
WHEN I HAVE YOUR WOUNDED

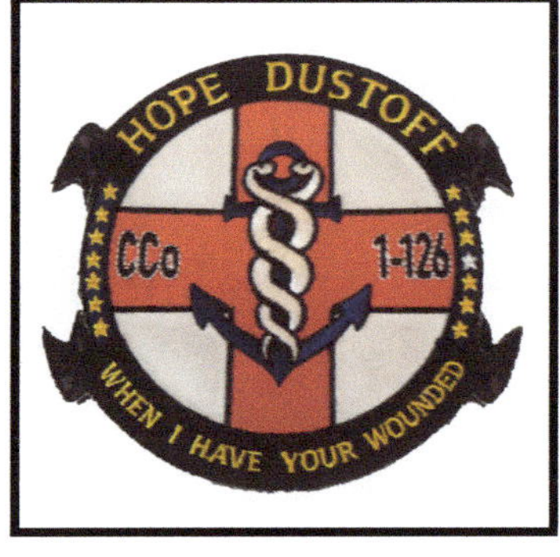
C CO 1/126
DUSTOFF

C CO 1/126
DUSTOFF

F Co 1-126TH MEDEVAC
FOR THE RIDE OF YOUR LIFE

F Co 1-126TH MEDEVAC
FOR THE RIDE OF YOUR LIFE

RHODE ISLAND
DUSTOFF
F

VICTORY
DUSTOFF
2

DET 2, F Co 1-126TH MEDEVAC
SO THAT OTHERS MAY LIVE

Co. 3-1-126th MEDEVAC (RI, DE, MD)
R.C. WEST
O.E.F. XI
In Chaos There is Hope

DELAWARE DUSTOFF
DET. 1, F. CO 1-126th

F Co 1-126th AVN
AIR AMBULANCE
FSMTI
OEF XI
SHINDAND, AFGHANISTAN
DUSTOFF

F CO 1-126
WITCH DOCTOR
OEF 12-13
MEDEVAC
cleared for flight closed for traffic

JUNGLE PENETRATING
OIR '18-'19
SPECIALISTS

TRAINWRECK MEDEVAC
2018-2019
OPERATION INHERENT RESOLVE

Battalion and Task Force patches

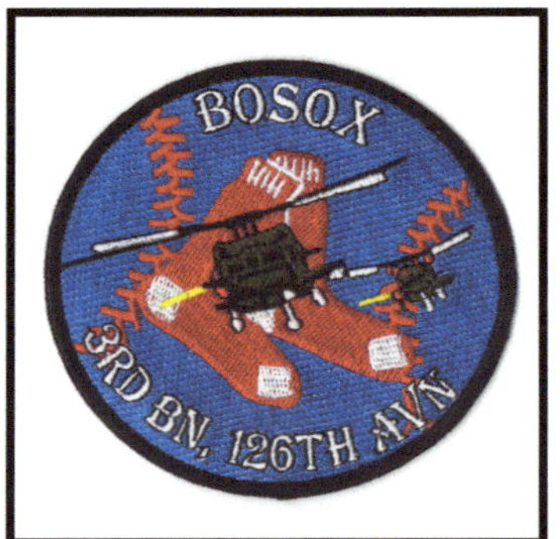

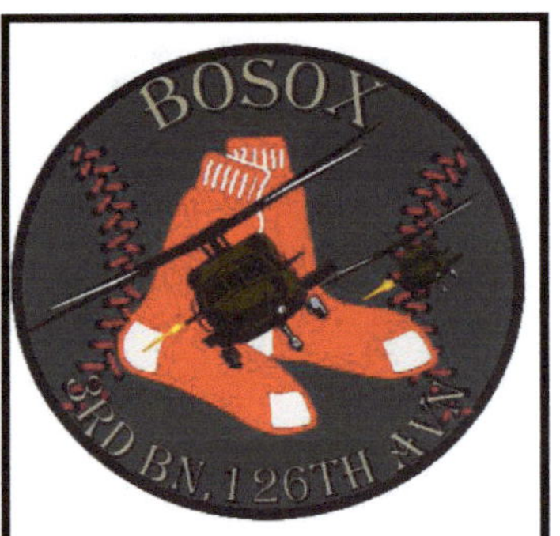

B Co. 3/126th AVN
HOOK'N TIME

CH-47D 86-01669
Hook'n Time
DALPORT LO KUCEK CAMPBELL

Hook'n Time

Baltimore Baby

B Co. 3/126TH AVN
HUMMER'S HOOKERS

B Co
3-126
DELIVERING THE FIGHT
KONG

B Co
3-126
DELIVERING THE FIGHT
KONG

OEF
2012-2013
KONG

OEF
2012-2013
KONG

TF GUNFIGHTER
TARIN KOWT
KONG

DET 1 B Co. 3-126 GSAB
EMPIRE BLIZZARD

DET 1 B Co. 3-126 GSAB
THE KONG

B Co. 3/126TH AVN
OEF
07-09
COMING TO A THEATER NEAR YOU

B Co. 3/126TH AVN
OEF
07-09
COMING TO A THEATER NEAR YOU

BRAVO CO. 3/126 AVN HVY
TF TIGERSHARK
"IN THRUST WE TRUST!"
JALALABAD AFGHANISTAN

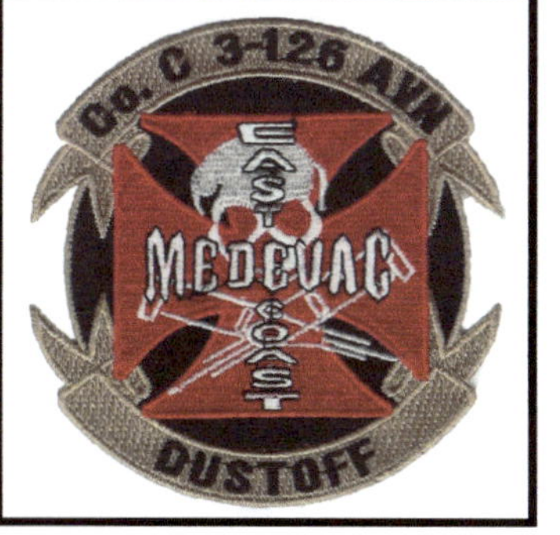
Co. C 3-126 AVN
EAST COAST
MEDEVAC
DUSTOFF

Co. C 3-126 AVN
OIF 05-07
MEDEVAC
SFOR 13-14
WITCHDOCTOR

WITCHDOCTORS
VT
DUSTOFF
MA
OND 10'-11'
CO C 3-126TH AVN

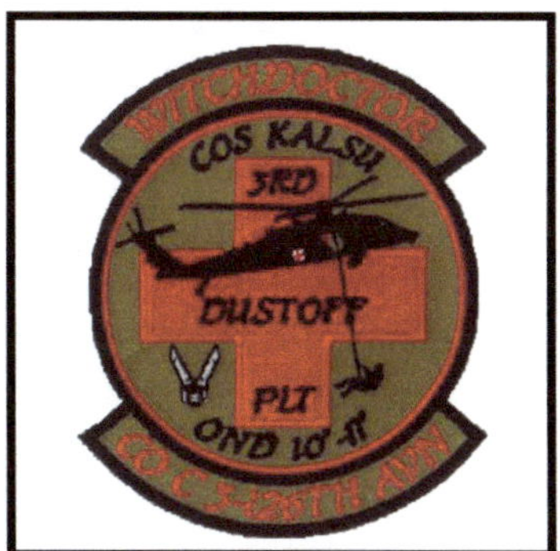
WITCHDOCTOR
COS KALSU
3RD
DUSTOFF
PLT
OND 10'-11'
CO C 3-126TH AVN

WITCH DOCTOR DUSTOFF
MASSACHUSETTS
DET 1 C CO. 3-126TH AVN

C CO 3-126 AVN
VT
MA
WITCH DOCTORS

Co. C3/126 AVN
BUSTIN' OURS
VT
MA
OIF-5
TO SAVE YOURS
DUSTOFF

Co. C3/126 AVN
BUSTIN' OURS
VT
MA
OIF-5
TO SAVE YOURS
DUSTOFF

Co. C3/126 AVN
BUSTIN' OURS
VT
MA
OIF-5
TO SAVE YOURS
DUSTOFF

KURDAGONIA DUSTOFF
OPERATION INHERENT RESOLVE
C CO 3-126
18-19

KURDAGONIA DUSTOFF
OPERATION INHERENT RESOLVE
C CO 3-126
18-19

DUSTOFF
THE BIZZ

IF YOUR NOT FIRST
1ST
A
Ω
YOUR LAST

C/3-126th AVN
VT
MA
volo obtinua

PATRIOT MEDEVAC
VT
MA CT
1ST
HH-60M
C CO 3-126TH AVN

C Company continued...

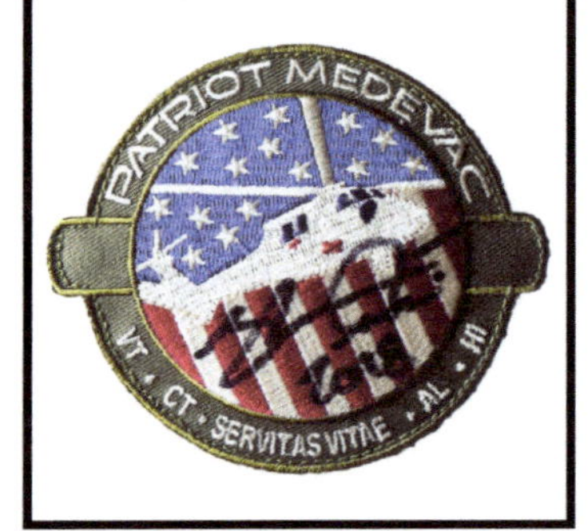

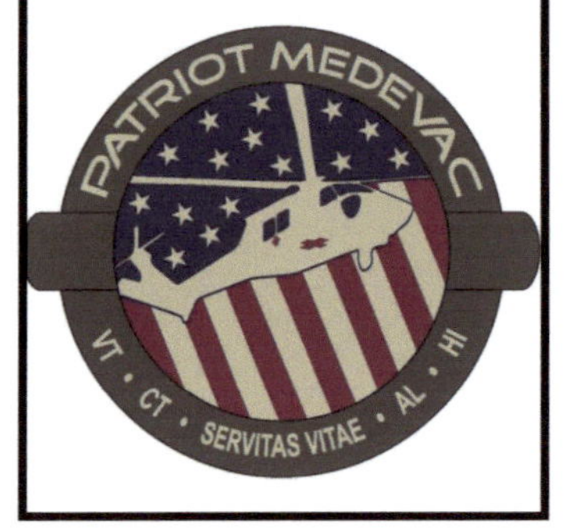

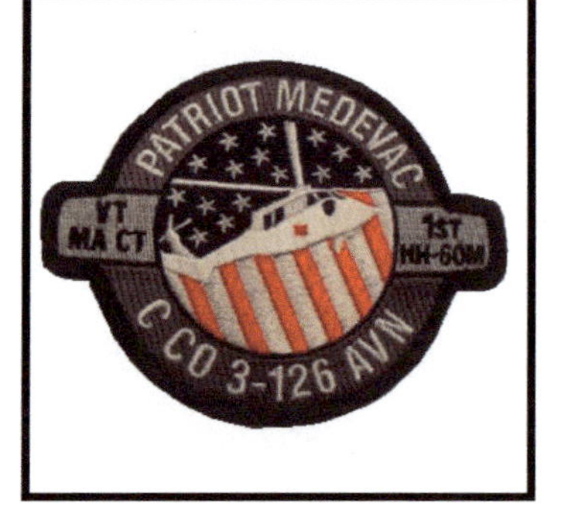

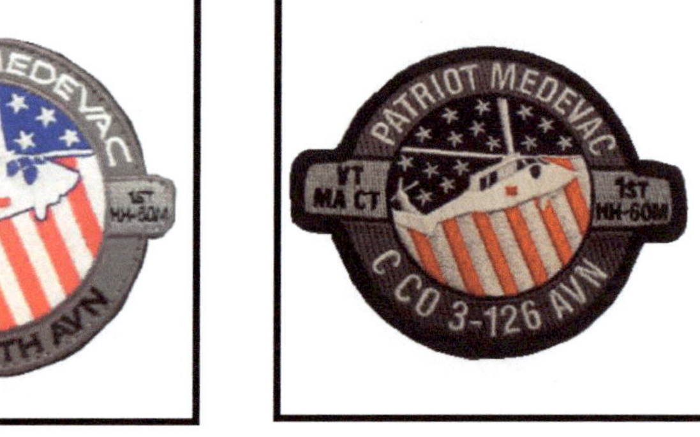

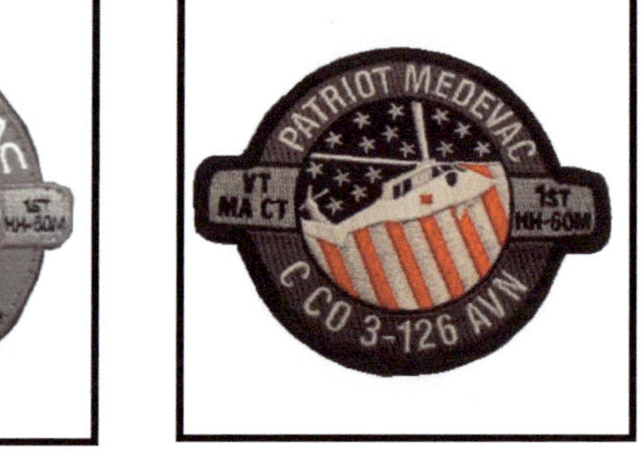

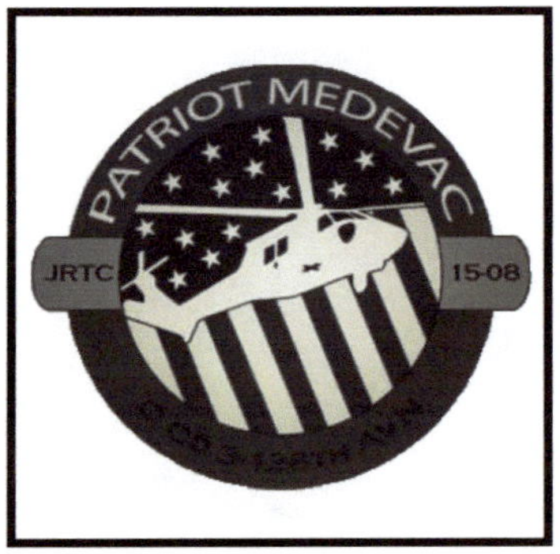

D Company 3-126 AVN

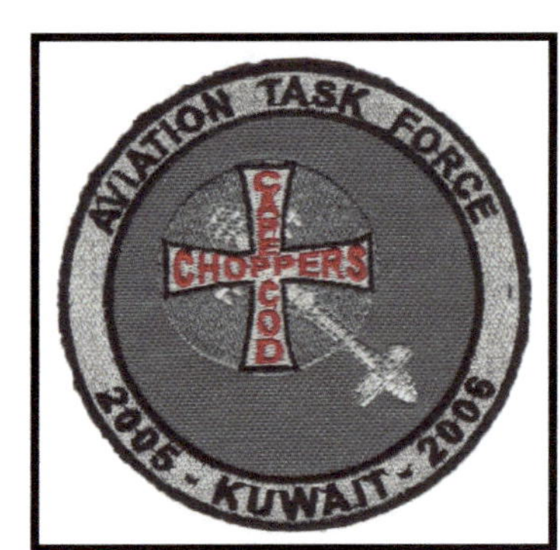

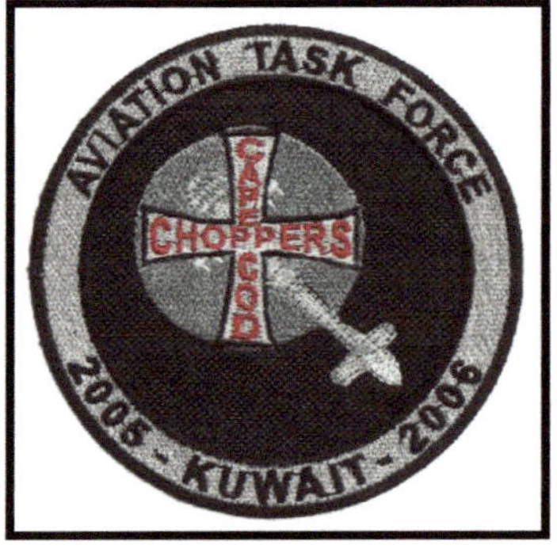

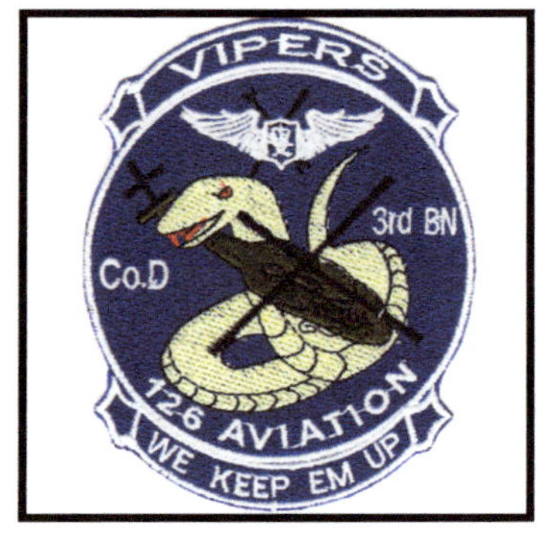

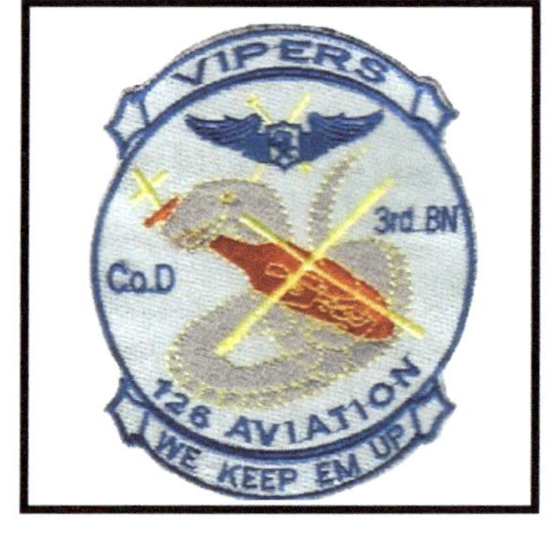

F Company 3-126 AVN

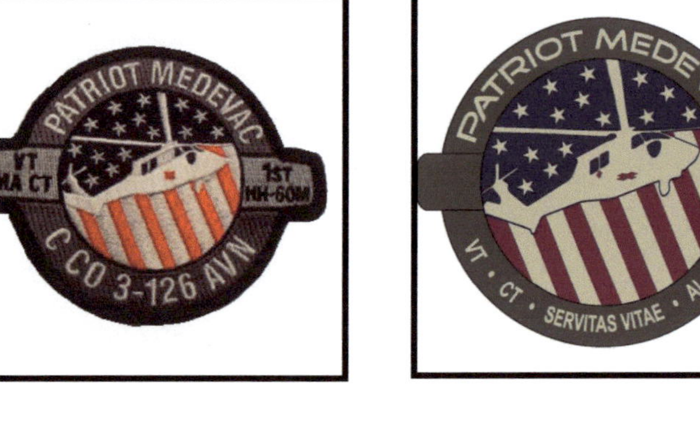

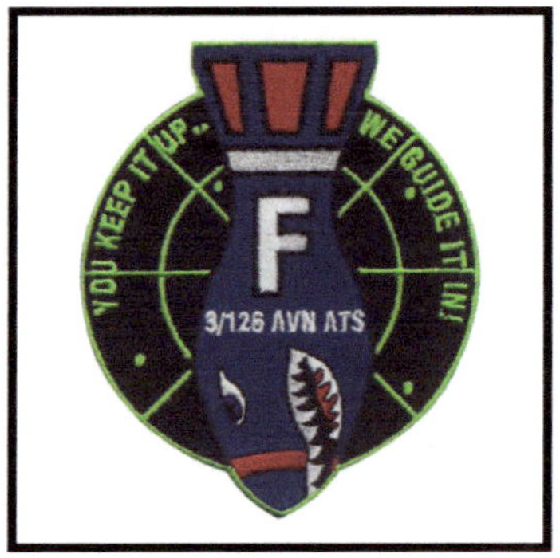

G3/126 GSAB
MOXIE
MEDEVAC
GIVES A HEALTHFUL LIFT!

G3/126 GSAB
MOXIE
MEDEVAC
GIVES A HEALTHFUL LIFT!

OFS 18-19
DWYER DUSTOFF
3-126
14
WAITING ON GUN

'ELEU DUSTOFF
D6/E6/G1 3-126 AVN REG
KE OLA MALU MAU

'ELEU DUSTOFF
D6/E6/G1 3-126 AVN REG
KE OLA MALU MAU

'ELEU DUSTOFF
D6/E6/G1 AVN
3/126 REG
KE OLA MALU MAU

1SN C CO 3-126TH
DET D CO 3-126TH
DUSTOFF
JRC OFS 18-19
"WHEN I HAVE YOUR WOUNDED"

DISTRICT DUSTOFF
VERY TALENTED
LOW FLYING
INFAMOUS

AFGHANISTAN
MAKING
YOU GREAT AGAIN
DC DUSTOFF
O F
S 18

DUSTOFF
OFS 18-19
THE LOST BOYS
G CO 3-126TH TF SHADOW

PRO PATRIA VIGILANS
COMMUNING WITH ANGELS 18-19

BOSOX
HHC, 3RD BN, 126TH AVN

BOSOX
HHC, 3RD BN, 126TH AVN

1st Battalion 131st Aviation Regiment

Assault Helicopter Battalion

Battalion and Task Force patches

A Company 1-131 AVN "DEATH ANGELS"

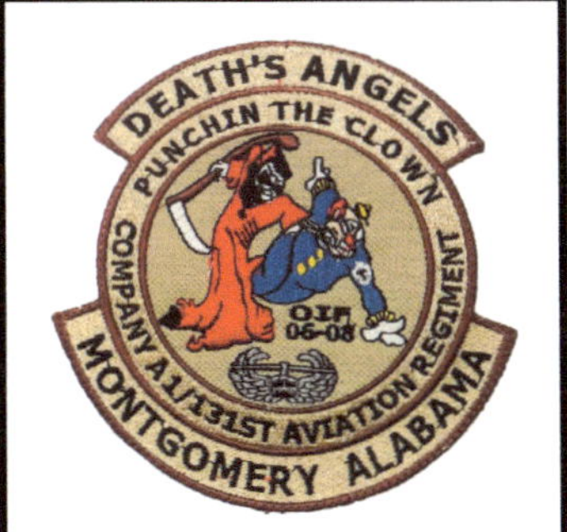   

1st Battalion 135th Aviation Regiment

Assault Helicopter Battalion

D Company 1-135 AVN "HAMMERHEADS"

AUTHOR'S NOTE: 1-135th AVN was an Attack Helicopter Battalion from 2001 until 2015 when the majority of National Guard and all Army Reserve attack helicopter units were converted to Assault Helicopter Battalions. As a result it has been difficult to locate or obtain patches or insignia for many of these units since the changeover took place. To see more 1-135 AVN patches please reference the Attack Helicopter Unit Patches book of this series.

Battalion and Task Force patches

B CO. BOOTLEGGERS
OIF 06-08
BALAD
HOOKERS OWN THE NIGHT

B CO 2-135 AVN
MULESKINNERS

B CO 2-135 AVN
MULESKINNERS

B CO 2-135 AVN
MULESKINNERS

B CO. 2-135 GSAB
DOOR GUNNER
DEATH IS AT THE DOOR
CH-47D

B CO. 2-135 GSAB
OEF XI-XII
★SHANK
★SAL
★KAF
"DUST IN THE WIND"

B CO 2-135 AVN · OIF 8 2019
KIDNAP FLIGHT

FORMERLY KNOWN AS 24th MED
2 135
OIF EMBRACE THE SUCK 06-08
Cutter

COMPANY C
Cutter
2-135TH GSAB

COMPANY C
Cutter
2-135th GSAB

C/2-135th GSAB
Cutter
OIF 06-08 DUSTOFF

C/2-135th GSAB
Cutter
OIF 06-08 DUSTOFF

DIRTY DUSTOFF
OND 10-11
Cheating Death One Flight At A Time
NE WI
C CO 2-135th GSAB

DIRTY DUSTOFF
OND 10-11
Cheating Death One Flight
NE WI
C CO 2-135th GSAB

Anywhere
Anytime
OND
10-11
2-/135th GSAB
DIRTY DUSTOFF

ARCHANGELS
NO GREATER LOVE

ARCHANGELS
NO GREATER LOVE

ADRENALINE
C CO. 2-135th GSAB

C CO 2-135TH GSAB
CA DUSTOFF

OFS 20-21
PIRATE DUSTOFF
KY NV
CA

OFS 20-21
PIRANCHE DUSTOFF
KY NV
CA

PIRATE DUSTOFF
KY CA NV
OFS 20-21

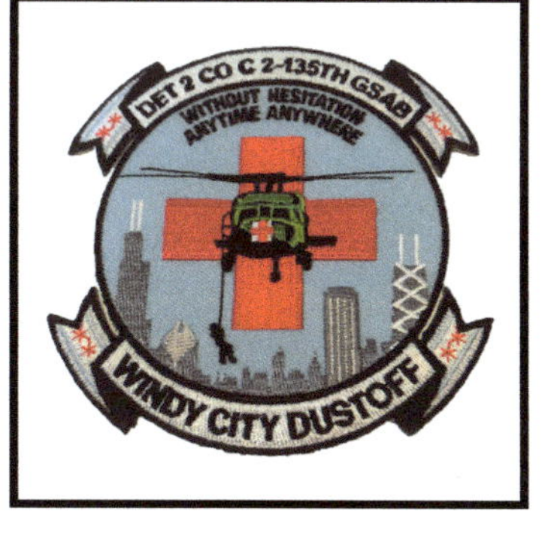

D Company 2-135 AVN "DAGGERS"   E Company 2-135 AVN "MARAUDERS"

F Company 2-135 AVN

F CO 2-135TH GSAB
TF DRAGONMASTER AFGHO
OEF
DIR 19-20
SUMO

F CO 2-135TH GSAB
TF DRAGONMASTER AFGHANISTAN
DIR 19-20
SUMO

CALIFORNIA
F CO 2-135TH AVN
DET 1
DUSTOFF

F CO 2-135TH AVN
BAYOU
DUSTOFF
BRING 'EM BACK ALIVE

F CO 2-135TH AVN
BAYOU
OEF 10-11
DUSTOFF

KANSAS COLORADO
2 135
G
SUBVENIO ALIPES

G/2 - 135th
ALL IN - OEF 14
CO
KS UT
UH-60
DUST OFF

G/2 - 135th
ALL IN
CO
KS UT
UH-60
DUST OFF

G/2 - 135th
ALL IN
CO
KS UT
UH-60
DUST OFF

FLY HARD
AND SAVE
LIVES

ALKUTRAZ
MEDEVAC
KANSAS COLORADO
2
G.Co
2-135th
2
10-11
QIF · OND

THIRD HERD G2-135
BAD MOON RISING

G CO. 2-135 GSAB (A/A)
Shindanta Afghanistan

1st Battalion 137th Aviation Regiment "PALE RIDERS"

Assault Helicopter Battalion

Battalion and Task Force patches

A Company 1-137 AVN "AVENGERS"

B Company 1-137 AVN "BLACK SHEEP" / "BLACK BARONS"

BEST OF THE BEST
1-137th
E Co.
WORK HORSE

IRON HORSE
HHC 1-137th
AVN REGT
"RIDE TOGETHER"

HHC 1-137 ASLTHB
IRON HORSE
World Wide Services

HHC 1-137TH AVN REGT
IRON HORSE
OIF '19

HHC 1-137TH AVN REGT
IRON HORSE
OIF '09

1st Battalion 140th Aviation Regiment

Assault Helicopter Battalion

WARHAWKS
B.CO.
1/140TH AVN BN (ASSLT)

WARHAWKS
B.co 1/140th AVN ASSLT

FOB SPEICHER OIF III
WARHAWKS
1/18 AIR CAV
B Co.
1/140 AVN

WARHAWKS
B Co.   1-140TH
AHB
ACCIPITRES BELLI SUMUS

OPERATION IRAQI FREEDOM
FOB SPEICHER
WARHAWKS
OIF III
2004-2005
B CO
1/140TH AVN

WARHAWKS
B.Co 1/140TH AVN ASSLT

C CO 1-140th AVN
OIF III
Ghost Warriors
04-05

COUGARS
C CO 1-140th AVN (ASLT)

COUGARS
BIBAMUS MORIENDUM EST

D Company 1-140 AVN "MAFIA"

E Company 1-140 AVN "OUTLAWS"

HHC 1-140 AVN "SHARK"

Battalion and Task Force patches

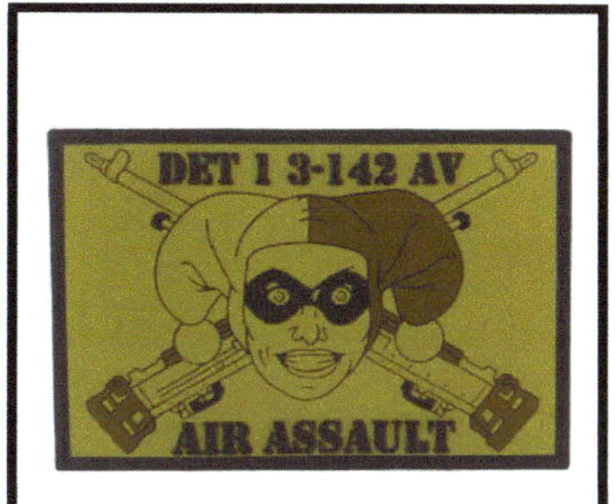

A CO.   3-142
ASSAULT

NY ARMY NATIONAL GUARD
ALPHA Co 3-142ND AHB
CCMRF

A CO. 3-142 AVN
O.I.F 2008 - 2009

A CO. 3-142 AVN
IT IS WHAT IT IS
O.I.F 2008-2009

A CO. 3-142 AVN
O.I.F 2008 - 2009

A CO. 3-142 AHB
'DS: 1
'MERICA   OEF '13 - '14

A CO. 3-142 AHB
'DS: 1
'MERICA   OEF '13 - '14

C Company 3-142 AVN "FURY"

Battalion amd Task Force patches

B Company 1-147 AVN "GRYPHONS" / "SILVERBACKS"

Co. C 1/147 C.A.B.
&
Command   Control
RES FIRME MITRE SCERE NESCIT

C CO 1-147TH MI ARNG
ALL IN

C CO. 1-147
C
CHAOS

SUSCIPIO PACIS PREPARING PRO BELLUM
1-147th AVN BN
D-Co AVUM
MIGHTY MERLINS

DELTA CO.1-147TH AVN
DRAGONMASTERS
BASRAH, IRAQ
OIF / NEW DAWN
2010-2011
W   MI
D CO.147Th AHB
"DRAGONMASTERS"

DC
D.CO 1-147TH AVN TAJI IRAQ
WE SCREW WE NUT WE BOLT
OIF 2010-11

HHC 1-147th AHB
OIF 10   OND 1
LYNCH AGMINIS

2nd Battalion 147th Aviation Regiment

Assault Helicopter Battalion

B 2-147 AVN ASSLT
RENEGADES

B 2-147 AVN ASSLT
RENEGADES

B 2-147 AVN ASSLT
RENEGADES

KENTUCKY
OSS
OIR
B CO
2-147
RENEGADES

BLUEGRASS
OSS
OIR
B CO
2-147
ASSAULT

B 2-147 AVN ASSLT
BLUEGRASS
RENEGADES

B 2-147 AVN ASSLT
RENEGADES
OEF/OIR 14-15

BLUEGRASS
TASK
FORCE
GUN
FIGHTER
SUMO

B
RENEGADES

FUERZAS COMANDO 2016
B
RENEGADES

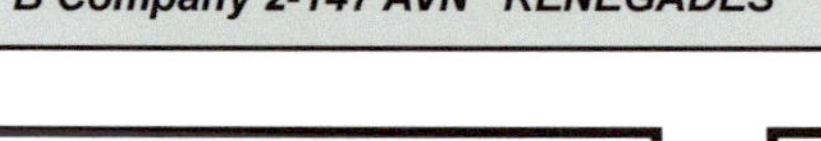

B CO 2-147
AVIATION   ASSAULT
KENTUCKY STRAIGHT
ARMY AVIATION
Bluegrass Renegades
KY NATIONAL GUARD
FRANKFORT, KENTUCKY USA

GRIFFINS
OEF
14-15
C CO 2-147 ASLT

C 147TH AIR ASSAULT
GRIFFINS

GRIFFINS
G CO. 2ND 147TH AVN

GRIFFINS
G CO. 2ND 147TH AVN

2019 - TF RAGNAR - 2020
IRAQ - OIR - JORDAN

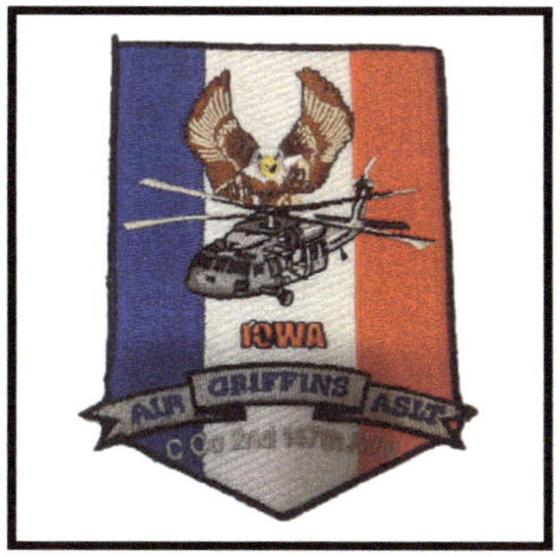

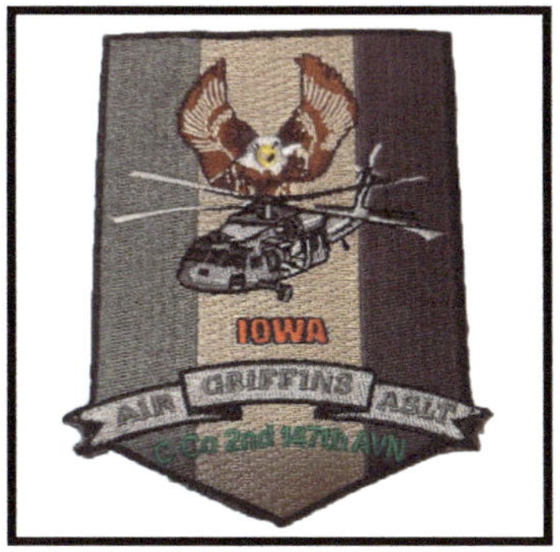

IOWA
AIR GRIFFINS ASLT
C CO 2nd 147th

IOWA
AIR GRIFFINS ASLT
C CO 2nd 147TH AVN

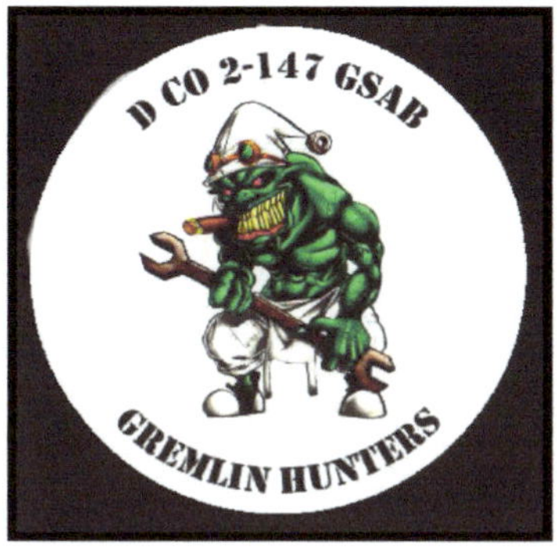

D CO 2-147 GSAB
GREMLIN HUNTERS

OPERATION INHERENT RESOLVE
TATANKA

TASK FORCE SHIELD
DELTA COMPANY
KY IA NJ MN NH TX MA
RI DE
OEF: KUWAIT
2014-2015

MT. NORTH ALMN.
THE FORGOTTEN
FUELERS

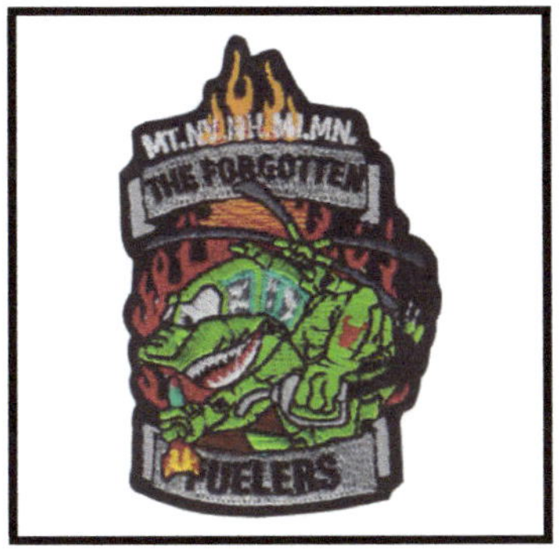

2nd Battalion 149th Aviation Regiment

General Support Helicopter Battalion

Battalion and Task Force patches

A Company 2-149 AVN "OUTRIDERS"

B Company 2-149 AVN "HOOKMASTERS"

E Company 2-149 AVN "OUTKASTS"

F Company 2-149 AVN "WATCHMEN"

HHC 2-149 AVN "MAVERICKS"

1st Battalion 150th Aviation Regiment "VANDALS"

Assault Helicopter Battalion

A Company 1-150 AVN "HOOLIGANS"

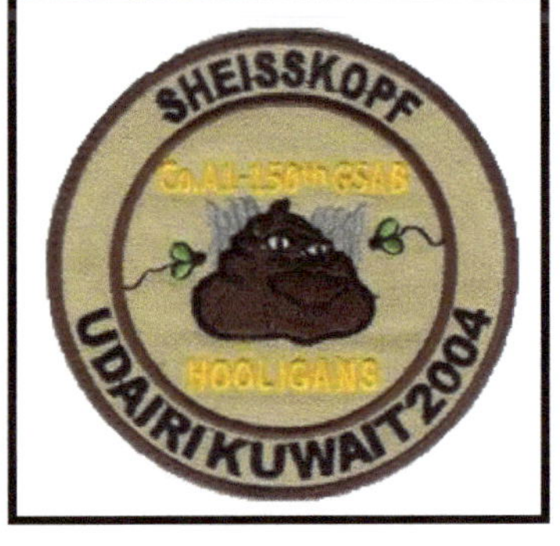    

B Company 1-150 AVN "MISFITS" / "BLACK SHEEP"

C Company 1-150 AVN "HAMMERHEADS" / "RIDGE RUNNERS"

D Company 1-150 AVN

E Company 1-150 AVN "JOKERS"

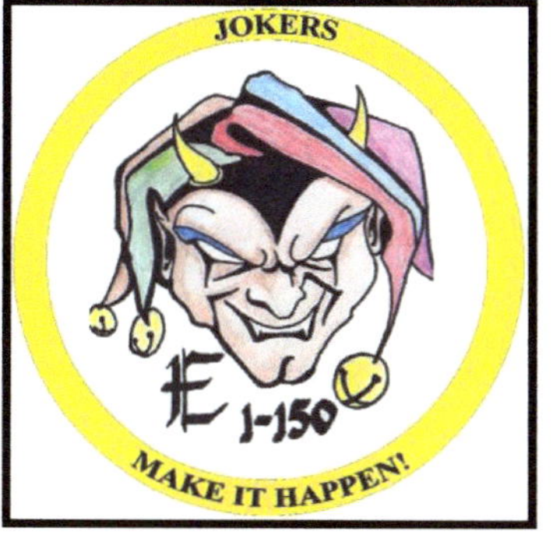

HHC 1-150 AVN

1st Battalion 158th Aviation Regiment

Assault Helicopter Battalion

B Company 1-158 AVN "OUTLAWS" / "BADGERS"

AIR SECURITY
SECRET   SERVICE

B COMPANY 1-158th AHB
BADGERS

AUTHOR'S NOTE: At the beginning of the Global War on Terror (9/11/2001) B Company 1-158th Aviation was an active-duty unit assigned to the 21st Cavalry Brigade at Fort Hood, TX. It is a unit with an interesting history beginning its post Vietnam life as the 175th Command Aviation Company ("OUTLAWS") assigned to the 6th Air Cavalry Brigade also at Fort Hood. After participating in Desert Storm and Operation Vigilant Warrior in 1994 the unit was transferred to the 21st Cavalry Brigade when the 6th Cavalry Brigade moved to Korea in 1996. Although the unit had been re-flagged as B Company 1-158th AVN while still assigned to the 6th Cavalry Brigade it was not widely known or referred to by that designation until its reassignment to the 21st CAV. During Operation Iraqi Freedom (OIF) B Company 1-158 AVN deployed to Balad Airbase, Iraq to support combat operations in 2006.

In 2015 B Company 1-158th AVN left the active roles with the disestablishment of the 21st Cavalry Brigade. Also in 2015 the US Army made the decision to remove the AH-64 from the Army Reserves fleet. As a result 7th Squadron 6th Cavalry based in Conroe, TX became 1-158th AVN and assumed the role of an Assault Helicopter Battalion.

Patches from the 175th CAC from the mid 90's timeframe.

7th Battalion 158th Aviation Regiment

General Support Aviation Battalion

7TH BATTALION
GHOST RIDERS
A
CO
158TH AVIATION REGIMENT

7TH BN
GHOST RIDERS
A
CO
158TH AVN REGT

7TH BATTALION
GHOST RIDERS
A
CO
158TH AVIATION REGIMENT

7TH BATTALION
GHOST RIDERS
A
CO
158TH AVIATION REGIMENT

7TH BATTALION
GHOST RIDERS
A
CO
158TH AVIATION REGIMENT

GHOST RIDERS
A
CO
AVIATION REGIMENT

A CO ROUGH RIDERS 7TH 158TH
MOVING THE FORCE

ALPHA COMPANY
CHINOOK D'S
BOEING CH-47
7-158TH AVN

A CO 7-158th AVN
VETIS

A CO 7-158th AVN
OEF9
GOMFM
VETIS

ROUGH RIDERS

ROUGH RIDERS
A CO. 7-158th AVN

ROUGH RIDERS
A CO. 7-158th AVN

SIKORSKY LIGHT UTILITY
STUTS
TRANSPORT SERVICE

SIKORSKY LIGHT UTILITY
TRANSPORT SERVICE

LANCERS
7TH BN
B CO
158TH AVN REGT

SPARTANS
με το η σε το
B/7-158th AVN

SPARTANS
B/7-158th AVN

SPARTANS
με το η σε το
B/7-158th AVN

SPARTANS
με το η σε το
B/7-158th AVN

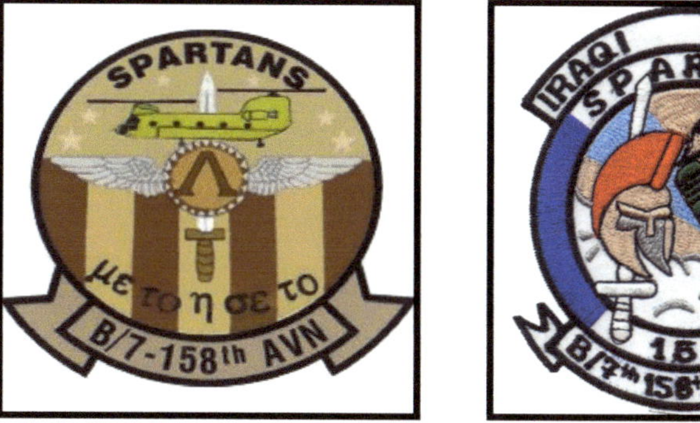

SPARTANS
με το η σε το
B/7-158th AVN

SPARTANS
με το η σε το
B/7-158th AVN

IRAQI FREEDOM
SPARTANS
184
B/7 156th AVN REGT

The Dirty Dime
LIBERTY
OEF XI-XII
B/7-158 AV Bagram Det
ZEPPELIN
DOGTOWN
XI XII
OEF
B/7-158 AVN

C/7-158 AVN REGT
SKILL NOT LUCK

C/7-158 AVN
OREGON DUSTOFF
1042

C/7-158 DSTF
SAINT DUSTOFF

6th PLT TRASH PANDAS
Zzzz
CAMP BUEHRING DUSTOFF
OSS/OIR 2022

TOWER 22 DUSTOFF
THE THREAT IS LOW BRO

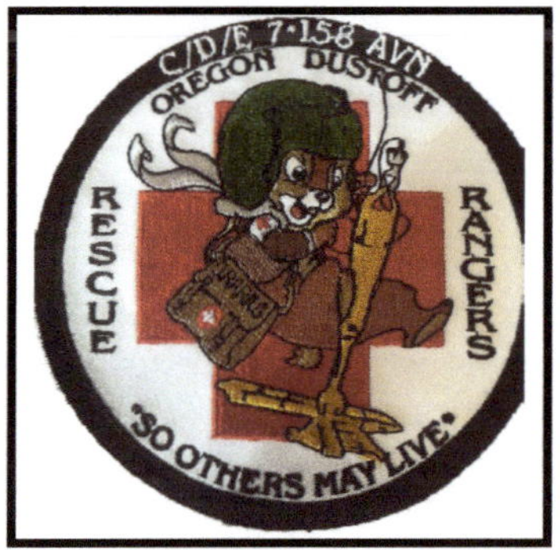

C/D/E 7-158 AVN
OREGON DUSTOFF
RESCUE
RANGERS
"SO OTHERS MAY LIVE"

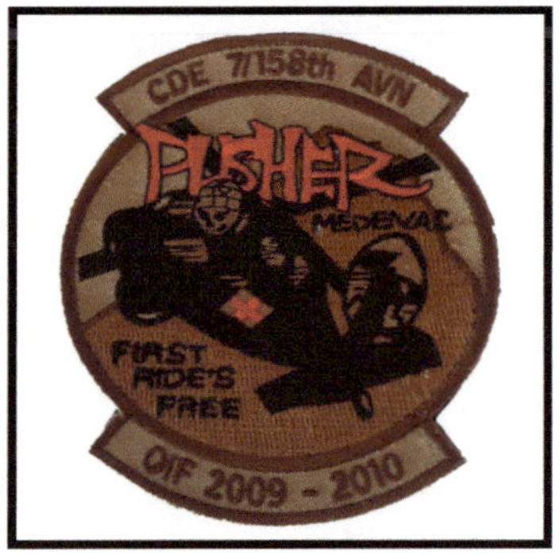

CDE 7/158th AVN
FISHER
MEDEVAC
FIRST RIDE'S FREE
OIF 2009 - 2010

MOONRACER MEDEVAC
PSAB OSS 21-22

SKALLYWAG
OIR 2021-2022
ENROUTE CRITICAL CARE NURSE

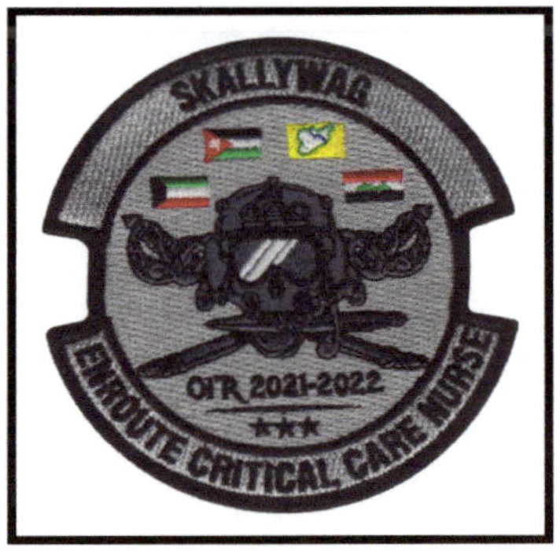

DELTA D/E-158th AVN DEMONS

F 7-158
SAINTS

F Co. 7-158 AVN REGT
SAINTS
DUST OFF

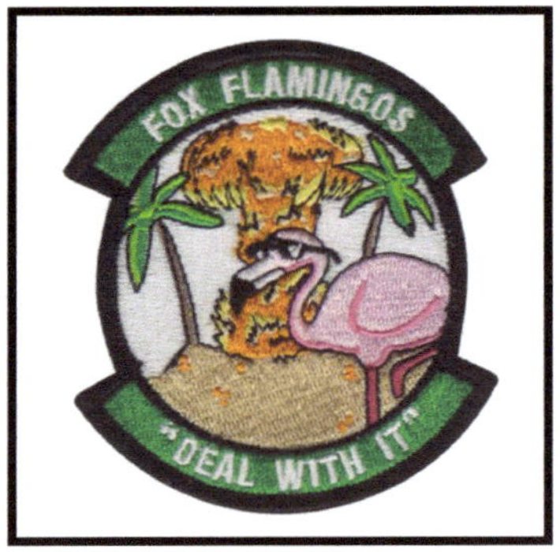

FOX FLAMINGOS
"DEAL WITH IT"

GOLF CO. 7-158
"Dustoff"
GUARDIANS

GOLF CO. 7-158
"Dustoff"
GUARDIANS

Battalion and Task Force patches

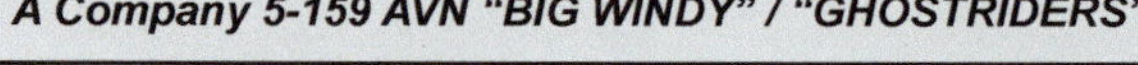

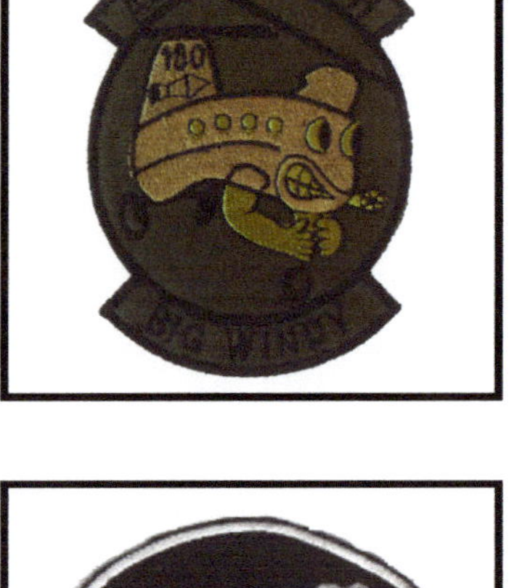

GHOSTRIDERS
UH 60
CLEARWATER FL

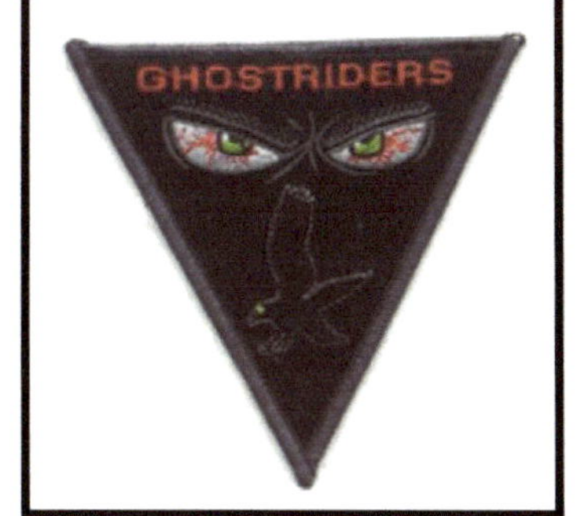
GHOSTRIDERS

GHOSTRIDERS

GHOSTRIDERS

GHOSTRIDERS

GHOSTRIDERS
ALPHA CO. 5/159
CLEARWATER FL

GHOSTRIDERS
ALPHA CO. 5/159
CLEARWATER FL

ROGUE
ALPHA CO. 5/159
CLEARWATER FL

SIKORSKY LIGHT UTILITY
TAXI SERVICE
CLEARWATER, FL
BOHICA

B/5 - 159th GSAB
FREIGHTTRAIN

BCo 5-159 AVIATION
FREIGHTTRAIN

B/5 - 159th GSAB
243
FREIGHTTRAIN

BCo 5-159 AVIATION
243
FREIGHTTRAIN

B/5 - 159th GSAB
243
FREIGHTTRAIN

BCo 5-159 AVIATION
FREIGHT TRAIN

BCo 5-159 AVIATION
FREIGHT TRAIN

TASKFORCE FREIGHTTRAIN
B&D CO, 5-159th AVN REGT

LIVIN' LARGE
P 11
IRAQ
MASH, ROSS, DOYLE

BC 05/159 AVN
DESERT HOOKERS

JAMES RIVER RAILROAD
B
5/159 FREIGHTTRAIN FELKER AAF

B Co
NIGHT TRAIN
LAYING TRACKS ALL NIGHT LONG

A KANDAHAR ORIGINAL
SOUTHERN
CARGO
OFS
16 17
RS

JAMES RIVER RAILROAD
B
5/159 FREIGHTTRAIN FELKER AAF

COWBOY DUSTOFF
C 5/159TH GSAB

COWBOY DUSTOFF
C Co 5-159
OEF
09-10
LET'ER BUCK!

COWBOY DUSTOFF
2015 2016
AFGHANISTAN

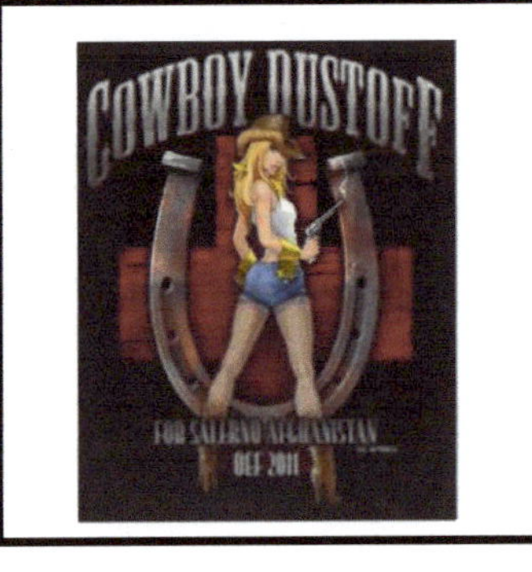
COWBOY DUSTOFF
FOB SALERNO AFGHANISTAN
OEF 2011

ROCKET CITY ROLLERS
SALERNO/OE
OEF IX-XI
COWBOY DUSTOFF
GAMBLING OUR LIVES TO SAVE YOURS

D Company 5-159 AVN "DARKWOLF" / "D BLOCK"

F Company 5-159 AVN "DEVIL RAY DUSTOFF"

G Company 5-159 AVN "DEVIL RAY DUSTOFF"

HHC 5-159 AVN "HEADHUNTERS"

Battalion and Task Force patches

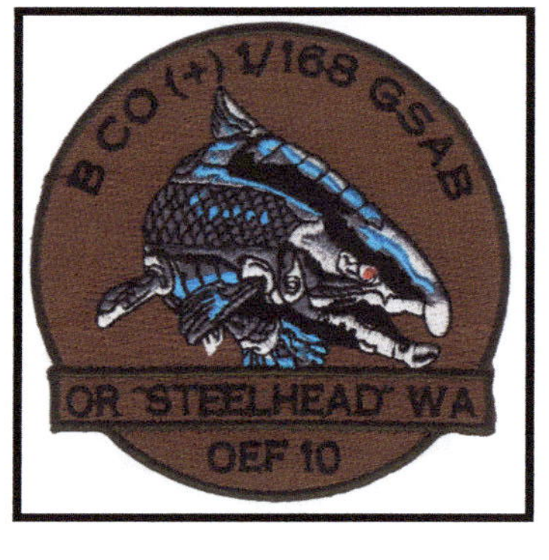    

C Company 1-168 AVN

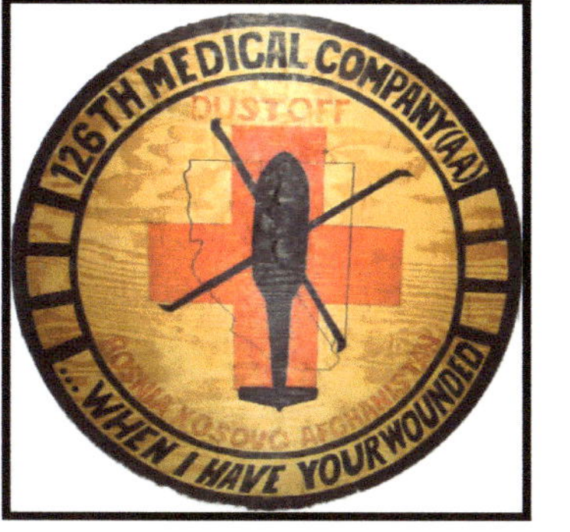

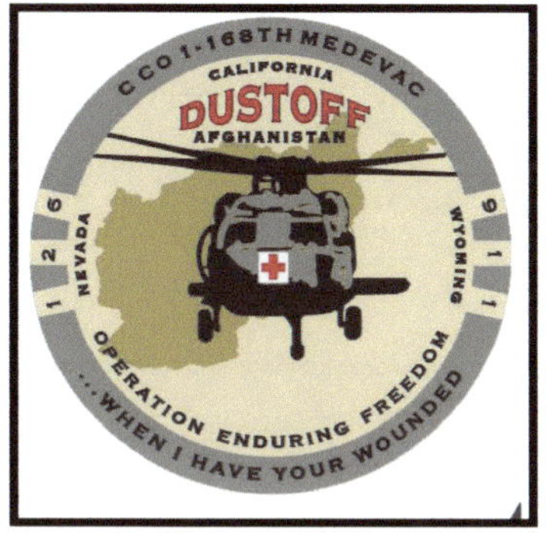

DUSTOFF
CALIFORNIA NEVADA WASHINGTON
C Co
AIR AMBULANCE 1-168

C CO DET 1 1-168 GSAB
WOLFPACK
WHEN I HAVE YOUR WOUNDED

C CO DET 1 1-168 GSAB
WOLFPACK
WHEN I HAVE YOUR WOUNDED

MILE HIGH MEDEVAC
D.U.S.T.O.F.F.
DET, 1 C CO 1/168TH

"When I Have Your Wounded"
COLORADO DUSTOFF

DET 2 Co C 1/168TH IDARNG
GUARDIAN MEDEVAC
16-19 OPERATION FREEDOM'S SENTINEL

DET 2 Co C 1/168TH IDARNG
GUARDIAN MEDEVAC
16-19 OPERATION FREEDOM'S SENTINEL

WHEN I HAVE YOUR WOUNDED
Rainier
DUSTOFF
Est 2012
DET 2 C 1-168TH

WHEN I HAVE YOUR WOUNDED
Rainier
DUSTOFF
DET 2 C 1-168TH

DET 2 C Co. 1-168th GSAB
DUSTOFF

GUARDIAN MEDEVAC
"WHEN I HAVE YOUR WOUNDED"
IDAHO ARMY NATIONAL GUARD A/168

DET 2 CO C 1/168TH IDARNG
GUARDIAN MEDEVAC
"WHEN I HAVE YOUR WOUNDED"

C CO 1-168 MEDEVAC
ES LO QUE ES
TEAM 2 CHINGADERAS OEF13-14

C CO 1-168 GSAB
VIOLENT RESCUE
MANBEARPIGS

Rainier Dustoff
HOIST OPERATOR'S UNION
LOCAL 1-168

E Company 1-168 AVN "ENFORCERS"

  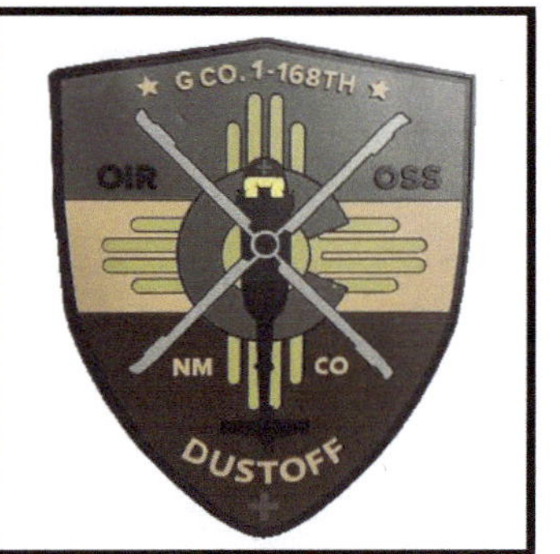  

HHC 1-168 AVN "HEAD HUNTERS"

1st Battalion 169th Aviation Regiment

General Support Aviation Battalion

Battalion patches

B Company 1-169 AVN

A Company 1-169 AVN

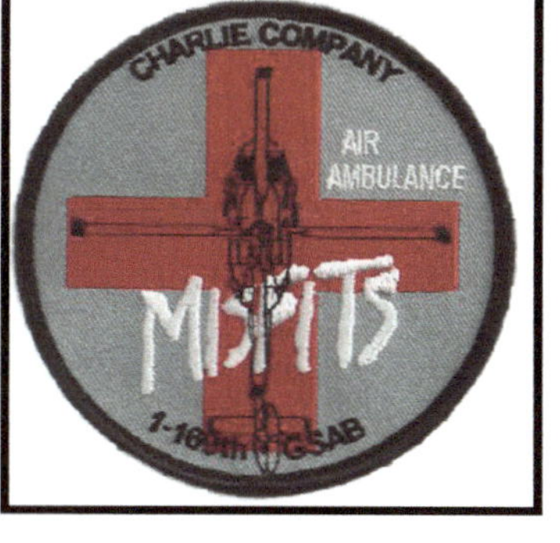    

D Company 1-169 AVN

F Company 1-169 AVN

1st Battalion 171st Aviation Regiment

General Support Aviation Battalion

Battalion and Task Force patches

B Company 1-171 AVN

  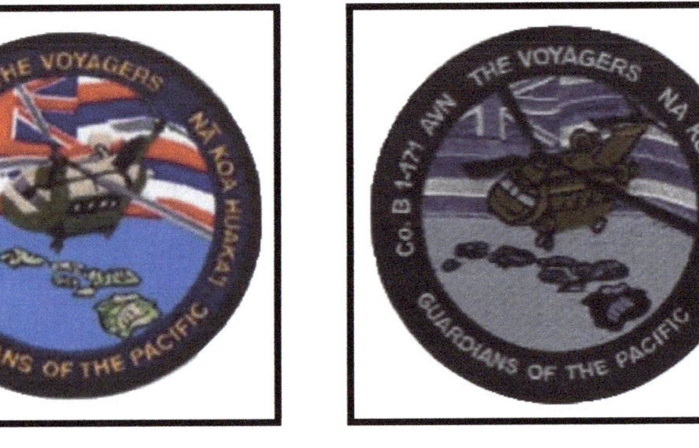  

C Company 1-171 AVN

 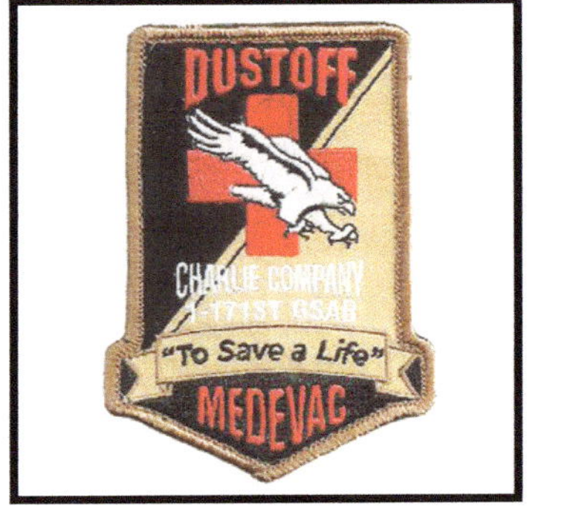  

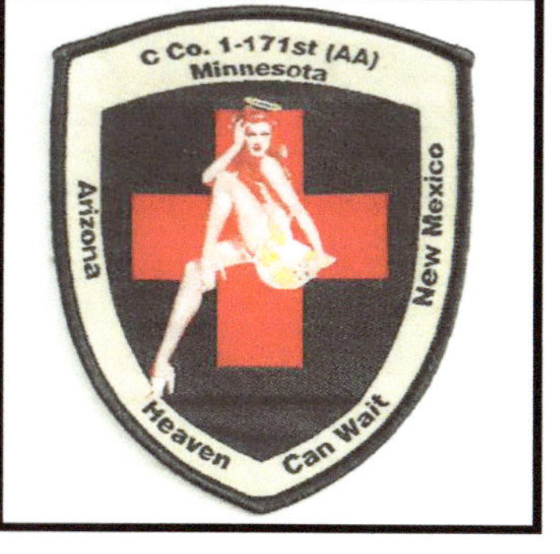
C Co. 1-171st (AA)
Minnesota
Arizona
New Mexico
Heaven Can Wait

WELCOME TO THE "NAM"
Co. C 1-171 GSAB
LOBO DUSTOFF
New Mexico • Arizona • Minnesota
STEALING FROM THE REAPER
NEW MEXICO, ARIZONA, & MINNESOTA
MEDEVAC

Co. C 1-171 GSAB
LOBO DUSTOFF
New Mexico • Arizona • Minnesota
"STEALING FROM THE REAPER"

Co. C 1-171 GSAB
LOBO DUSTOFF
New Mexico • Arizona • Minnesota
STEALING FROM THE REAPER

THE LOUDER YOU SCREAM
C.Co 1-171
DUSTOFF
THE FASTER WE COME

WOLFPACK
FM32
BUT DID YOU DIE?

4TH FSMP
C CO. 1-171
MS NJ NY WY
OFS 2019 OR5
DO AS YOU'RE TOLD!
FURY DUSTOFF

171
Det 1, C Co

DRAGON DUSTOFF
MS • NJ • NY • WY
C/1-171st

DRAGON DUSTOFF
MS • NJ • NY • WY
C/1-171st

DRAGON DUSTOFF
MS • NJ • NY • WY
OPS COMMO
C/1-171st

Dungeons &
MS NJ NY WY
Dragon Dustoff

C-1-171 5TH PLATOON
KHALEESI DUSTOFF

C-1-171 5TH PLATOON
KHALEESI DUSTOFF

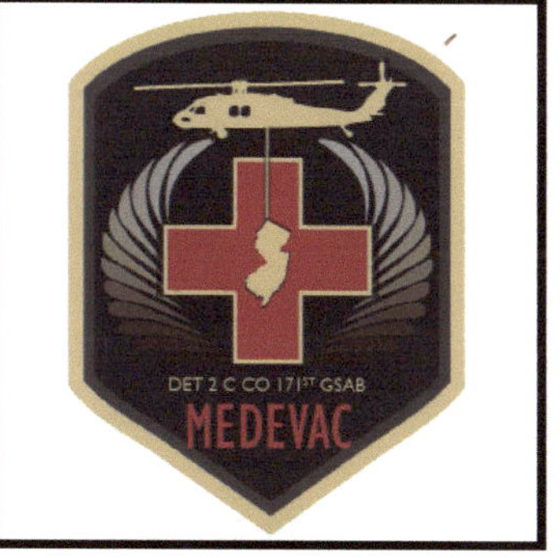
DET 2 C CO 171st GSAB
MEDEVAC

D Company 1-171 AVN

F Company 1-171 AVN

HHC 1-171 AVN "BULLDOGS"

1st Battalion 183rd Aviation Regiment

B Company 1-183 AVN "FALCONS"	C Company 1-183 AVN

AUTHOR'S NOTE: The 1st Battalion 183rd Aviation Regiment until 2015 had been an Attack Helicopter battalion flying the AH-64 Apache. As part of the Army's aviation restructuring inititive they traded in their Apaches for UH-60 Black Hawks and reformed as an Assault Helicopter Battalion. Unfortunately, we were only able to locate these two patches from after the redesignation. To see more 1-183rd patches please reference the Attack Helicopter Unit Patches book from this series.

Battalion and Task Froce Patches

A Company 1-185 AVN

B Company 1-185 AVN "DRAGONS"

C Company 1-185 AVN

D Company 1-185 AVN "DRAGONS" / "WORKHORSE"

E Company 1-185 AVN

Battalion and Task Force Patches

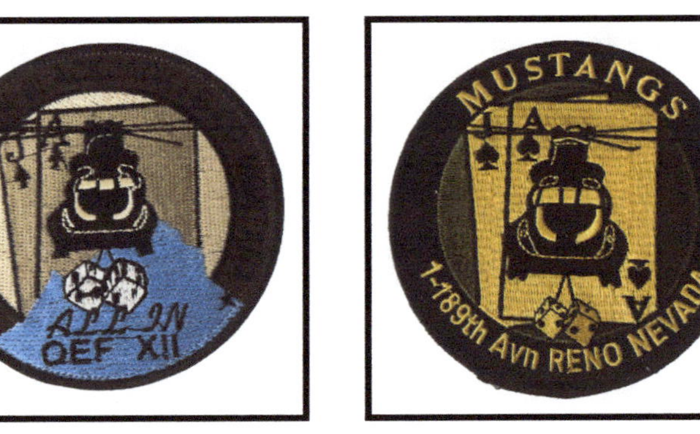

MONTANA DET 1 CO C 1-189TH GSAB AVIATION
7
3 77
VIGILANTE DUSTOFF

MONTANA DET 1 CO C 1-189TH GSAB AVIATION
7
3 77
VIGILANTE DUSTOFF

MONTANA DET 1 CO C 1-189TH GSAB AVIATION
7
3 77
VIGILANTE DUSTOFF

BLACKSHEEP DUSTOFF
HH-60M
DET 1 CO C 1-189 GSAB

C CO 1-189
OND IRAQ

C CO 1-189
OND IRAQ

C CO 1-189
OND IRAQ

DUSTOFF
C CO
1 189
HH-60M

DUSTOFF
C CO
1 189
HH-60M

HOMESKOOL
OIR 17-18
Drop us a line
DUSTOFF

C CO 1/189TH AVN
Homeskool
DUSTOFF WEST

MISFITS
C CO. 1-189th GSAB

MISFIT MEDEVAC
OFS 18-19
2ND TO NONE

C CO 1/189TH GSAB
SD MT
MIDNIGHT MEDEVAC

C CO 1/189TH GSAB
SD MT
MIDNIGHT MEDEVAC

F Company 1-189 AVN

G/1-189 MEDEVAC
The Happiest Place on Earth

WARRIOR DUSTOFF
D4/E5/G1
AVN
1/189TH
REG
KAHU O KE OLA

WARRIOR DUSTOFF
AVN
REG
KAHU O KE OLA

CALL KENNY LOGGINS CAUSE YOU'RE IN THE
DANGER ZONE!
G/1-189
DUSTOFF

FORTES FORTUNA ADJUVAT XIVII
CREWCHIEF
G 1-189
OREGON DUSTOFF

FORTES FORTUNA ADJUVAT XIVII
PILOT
G 1-189
OREGON DUSTOFF

FORTES FORTUNA ADJUVAT XIVII
FLIGHT PARAMEDIC
G 1-189
OREGON DUSTOFF

FORTES FORTUNA ADJUVAT XIVII
LEGACY
G 1-189
OREGON DUSTOFF

FORTES FORTUNA ADJUVAT XIVII
PILOT IN COMMAND
G 1-189
OREGON DUSTOFF

TASK FORCE DUSTOFF
MT
OR
MA

TASK FORCE DUSTOFF
MT
OR
MA

2nd Battalion 211th Aviation Regiment

General Support Aviation Battalion

Battalion and Task Force patches

RUMRUNNERS
A-2-211
OIF 09-10
GOT RUM?

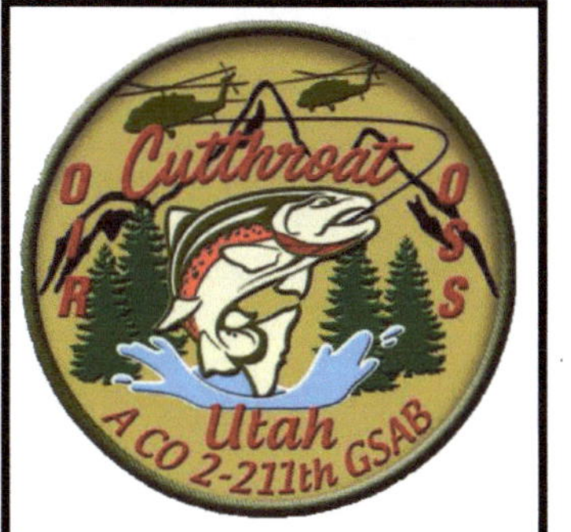

Cutthroat
O
O
R
S
S
Utah
A CO 2-211th GSAB

Cutthroat
O
O
R
S
S
Utah
A CO 2-211th GSAB

Cutthroat
A CO 2-211th GSAB
Utah

Cutthroat
A CO 2-211th GSAB

B CO 2-211TH AVN
ALL NIGHT LONG

B Co 2-211 GSAB
IOWA
OPERATION NEW DAWN
ALL NIGHT LONG

B Co 2-211 GSAB
IOWA
OPERATION NEW DAWN
ALL NIGHT LONG

B Co. 2-211TH YETIS
33
Illgitimis Non Carborundum

C CO. 2-211 GSAB
OEF 2012-2013
NORTHSTAR DUSTOFF

C Co. 2-211th Avn (AA)
North Star Dustoff

North Star Dustoff

C CO. 2-211TH (AA) TF RUMOR
MULTI-THEATER
OIF 08-10   OEF 09-11
MEDEVAC
North Star   Dustoff

C Co. 2-211th (AA)
OIF 08-10
Minnesota
Iowa
North Star   Dustoff

NORTHSTAR DUSTOFF
C CO. 2-211TH GSAB

NORTHSTAR DUSTOFF
C CO. 2-211 TH GSAB

NORTHSTAR DUSTOFF
C CO. 2-211TH GSAB
REMEMBER 967
05 DECEMBER 2019

NORTHSTAR   DUSTOFF
"WHEN I HAVE   YOUR WOUNDED"
OIF 08-09   OEF 11-12
OEF 12-13   OEF 15-16
C CO. 2-211   C Co. 1-171

NORTHSTAR DUSTOFF
MED HAWK
C CO. 2-211   C CO. 1-171

THE DUST REAM COFFEE SHOP
C Co. 2-211TH GSAB

NON
G 211
IN NOSTRUM VIGILO

KANSAS
DET. 2 C CO 2/211th MED

DELTA CO 2-211TH GSAB
JORDAN
IRAQ
KUWAIT
SYRIA
LUBIN' & SCREWIN' SINCE 1979

D CO 2-211TH GSAB
CLUB BUEHRING
TF WARHORSE 2018-2019

G CO. DET 1 2/211 MEDEVAC
WASATCH DUSTOFF

G CO. DET 1 2/211 MEDEVAC
WHEN I HAVE YOUR WOUNDED
WASATCH DUSTOFF

G CO. DET 1 2/211 MEDEVAC
WASATCH DUSTOFF

COWBOY DUSTOFF
G2-211th AVN

COWBOY DUSTOFF
2015 2016
AFGHANISTAN

ALASKA
The Last Frontier
AIR AMBULANCE

G CO. 2-211
ALASKA AIR AMBULANCE
DUSTOFF

AKARNG MEDEVAC
DUSTOFF
UT ALLI VIVANT

2nd Battalion 224th Aviation Regiment

Assault Helicopter Battalion

Battalion Patches

A Company 2-224 AVN "PUNISHERS"

B Company 2-224 AVN "BEAST"

C Company 2-224 AVN "RAVEN ASSAULT"

8th Battalion 229th Aviation Regiment

Assault Helicopter Battalion

Battalion Patches

B Company 8-229 AVN

C Company 8-229 AVN

E Company 8-229 AVN "EAGLES"

1st Battalion 230th Aviation Regiment

Assault Helicopter Battalion

A Company 1-230 AVN "MOONSHINE"

B Company 1-230 AVN

A Company 1-230 AVN "MOONSHINE"

B Company 1-230 AVN

C Company 1-230 AVN

C Company 1-230 AVN

AUTHOR'S NOTE: *The companies of 1-230th AVN of the Tennessee Army National Guard, were previously known as the Air Troops of the 1st Squadron 230th Armored Cavalry Regiment. They operated OH-58D Kiowa Warriors and AH-64 Apaches at various times. As has been noted previously this unit was one of many that converted to another role and turned in their attack helicopters in exchange for UH-60s. Unfortunately, these patches were the only ones we could find for this unit after its conversion.*

B Company 2-238 AVN "RIVER CITY HOOKERS"

C-CO 2-238
BRICKYARD DUSTOFF

HOOSIER DUSTOFF
CO.C 2/238TH
QUISQUAM
USQUAM
Indy

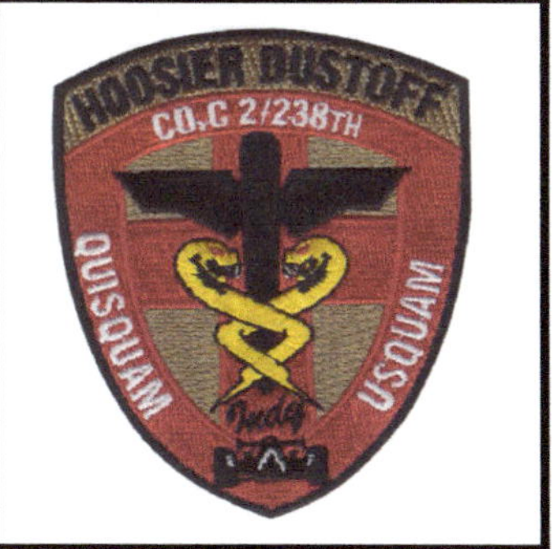
HOOSIER DUSTOFF
CO.C 2/238TH
QUISQUAM
USQUAM
Indy

HOOSIER DUSTOFF
CO.C 2/238th
QUISQUAM
USQUAM
Indy

HOOSIER DUSTOFF
CO.C 2/238TH
QUISQUAM
USQUAM
Indy

HOOSIER DUSTOFF
QUISQUAM
USQUAM
Indy

HOOSIER DUSTOFF
CO.C 2/238TH
QUISQUAM
USQUAM

TASK FORCE DUSTOFF
C&D CO. 2/238th
OIF '07-'09
QUISQUAM
USQUAM
Indy

TASK FORCE DUSTOFF
C&D CO. 2/238th
OIF '07-'09
QUISQUAM
USQUAM
Indy

TASK FORCE DUSTOFF
C&D CO. 2/238th
OIF '07-'09
QUISQUAM
USQUAM
Indy

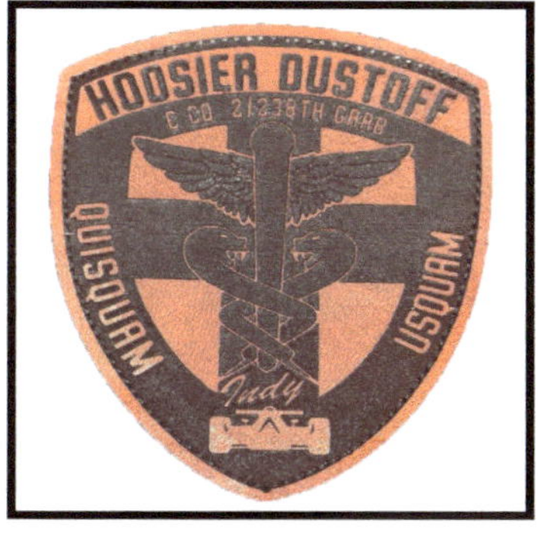
HOOSIER DUSTOFF
C CO. 2/238TH GARB
QUISQUAM
USQUAM
Indy

MILE HI DUSTOFF
CO.C 2/238th
QUISQUAM
USQUAM

MILE HI DUSTOFF
CO.C 2/238th
QUISQUAM
USQUAM

MILE HI DUSTOFF
CO.C 2/238th
QUISQUAM
USQUAM

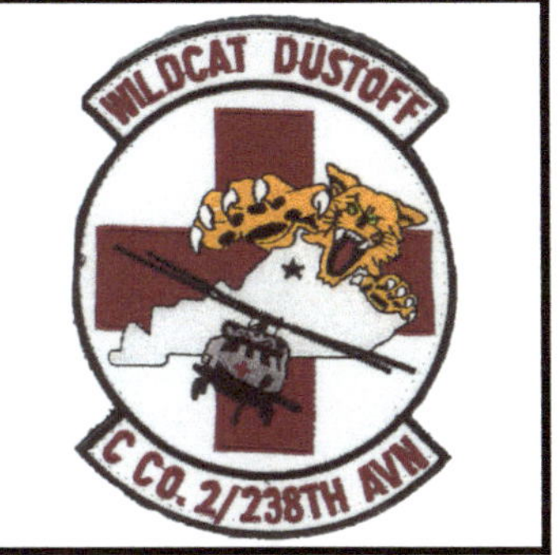
WILDCAT DUSTOFF
C CO. 2/238TH AVN

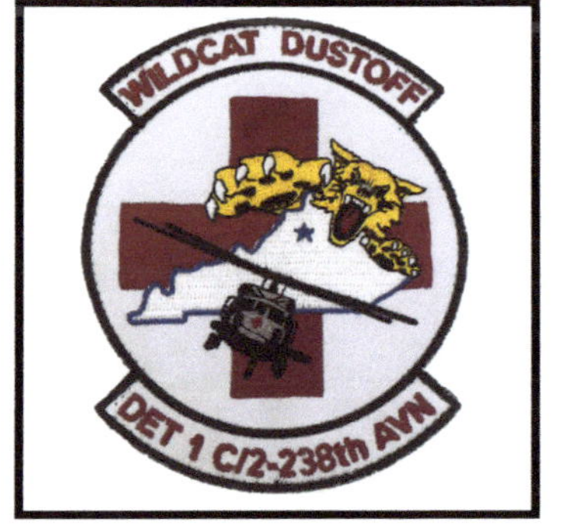

F Company 2-238 AVN

3rd Battalion 238th Aviation Regiment

General Support Aviation Battalion

Battalion and Task Force patches

A Co. 3-238 CSAB
SILVERBACKS

A CO 3-238 AVN
NO ONE WANTS TO
PLAY WITH US
MISFITS

A CO 3-238 AVN
NO ONE WANTS TO
PLAY WITH US
MISFITS

B CO. 3/238TH GSAB
A HOUSE DIVIDED
O M
ENEMIES SINCE 1935
ONLY WAR COULD UNITE US

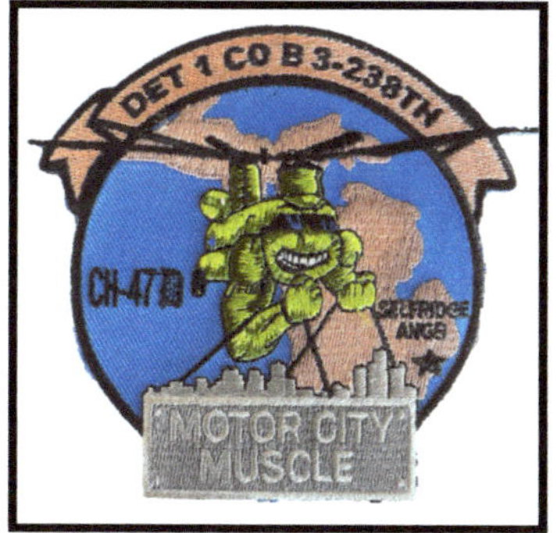

MIDWEST HOOKERS
TURNING HEADS AND BEARDS
O M
WE AID THE WORLD b OEF 20??
B CO. 3/238TH GSAB

DET 1 CO B 3-238TH
CH-47D
SELFRIDGE ANGB
MOTOR CITY MUSCLE

B CO. 3-238TH AVN
VALUS VELOX PROCINCTU

MISFIT
COMPANY B 3-238TH GSAB

OUTKAST
K
OIR 20/21
K
TF GAMBLER

K
TF GAMBLER
OUTKAST
OIR 20/21
K

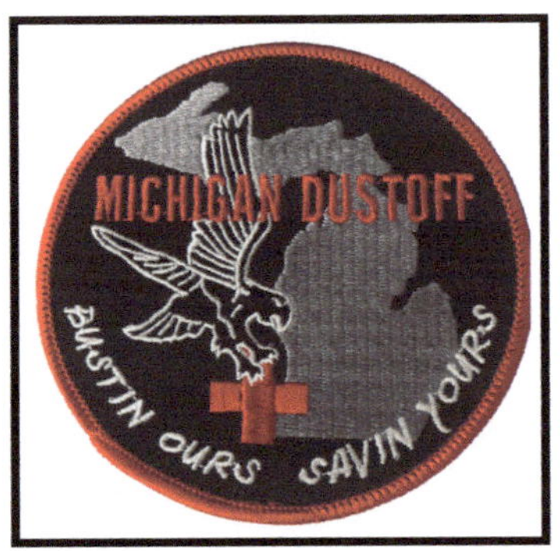

G Company 3-238 AVN

Battalion and Task Force Patches

Co A 1-244th AVN
AIR ASSAULT

Co A, 1-244th AVN
SUPERMEN

ALPHA
ANDYGATORS
A Co 1-244th AHB

B Co 1-244th AVIATION
FROM DUSK TILL DAWN

B Co 1-244th AVIATION
FROM DUSK TILL DAWN

B Co 1-244th AVIATION
OPERATION INHERENT RESOLVE

Co C 1-244th AHB
PRIVATEERS
El Marque De La
FLORIDA

C CO 1-244TH AVN BN
FROM DUSK TO DAWN

TULSA
LUNAR
LORDS OF DARKNESS
C CO. 1-244 AHB

Lords of
Lunar
Darkness
C Co 1-244 ASSAULT

Lunar
C Co 1-244 ASSAULT
Lords of Darkness

C CO 1-244 AVN REG
LORDS OF DARKNESS

D CO 1-244th AVN
IRONMAN
MAINTENANCE

TASK FORCE VOODOO OIROSS
2017
2018
HHC 1-244TH

ROGUE
TF VOODOO
COMMUNICATIONS

2nd Battalion 285th Aviation Regiment

Assault Helicopter Battalion

A Company 2-285 AVN

B Company 2-285 AVN

C Company 2-285 AVN   D Company 2-285 AVN "ROADRUNNERS"

CONTRIBUTORS

There is no way that this book could have ever been made without the help of a lot of other people. Below is a list of some of the many folks who helped in getting me images or actual patches to be included in this project. Unfortunately some of these folks are no longer with us. This hobby will be poorer in their absence but we are all richer for having known them. Everything good in this book is because of these fine folks.

THANK YOU!

Aeroemblem, Keith Alan, Apache Warrior Foundation, Aviator Gear, Emil Balusek (RIP), David Barber, Paul Belobrajdic, Joe Belsha, Keith Benner, Steve Boras, Perry Bowden, Jack Brink, Steve Bull, Brian Carbone, Clint Chamberland, Ashlie Christian, Jeff Crownover, Dan Cruz, Tim Dolifka (RIP), Kevin Dishner, Chris Dixon, Al Dupre, Rod Dwyer, Daniel Flores, Geoff Florom, Bill Fox, Carl Fox, Jake Gaston, Nick Hatchel, Glen Hees, Mark Hough, Britton Howell, Aaron Joe, David Johns, Micah Johnson, Eric Jurarez, Levi Kaiser, Christopher Koth, Aaron Krupa, Billy L LeJeune, Keith Lindsey, Jef Litvin, CW4 Matt Lourey (RIP), Ryan Madar, Angelica Maria, Jim McLean, Herbert McTacops, Fox Mike, Russ Mixon, Samuel Mo, CV Nance, Ryan Nelson, Matthew Norbury, Robert Reardon, Alec Record, Steve Reynolds, Lea A. Rhinehart, Jason Richards, Angelo Rickert, Jennifer Gruber Roach, Tom Rude, Alan Sanders, Steven Sandoval, Borna Skedel, Keith Stilwell, Rocky Sudduth, Brian Serna, Mark Shaw, Carl Smith, Dustin Smith, Keith Snyder, Jay Son, Shaun Steines, Tad Stuart, Shaun Thurman, Trident's Edge Designs, Jeffrey Trombly, US Company, Pascal Vermeersch, Seth Vieux, Andy Wilson, Alan Woods, and Vance Zemke

"HEY, WHERE"S MY PATCH?"

If your patch or your unit was inadvertently left out of this book or we got something wrong, we apologize. We want to make this book as accurate as possible, so if you would be nice enough to send an image and a short explanation of the patch to dngrpig@ gmail.com, we will make sure it's included in future editions and your name will be added to the list of contributors.
THANK YOU FOR YOUR COMMITMENT TO PRESERVING THE HISTORY OF ARMY AVIATION!

.